KEY STUDY VALUES

Below are the key values behind reading the bible like a human being. The phrases are intended in pithy, memorable form so you can easily remember and apply them:

EXPERIENCING JESUS
We study to experience the human Jesus personally, not to learn what to believe or how to behave.

DON'T BE HALF-BRAINED
Your rational brain knows God, your emotional brain experiences him. You need to study with both.

EMOTIONS HAVEN'T CHANGED
Human brains and emotions haven't changed in 2000 years, so applying my life experience to scripture can help me understand it.

NO MAGIC JESUS
We don't make up 'Magic Jesus' explanations to avoid acknowledging his humanity. (We also don't explain away the miracles in the bible to downplay his divinity!)

MAKE STUFF UP!
We can use imagination to fill in the missing details without needing to get every fact exactly right, because we aren't making doctrine. Our emotional brain insights don't replace sound doctrine, they are tested by it.

ON THE COVER...

In this view of the Sea of Galilee, taken from the traditional site of the Sermon on the Mount, you can see the monasteries of Capernaum nestled along the shoreline a mile away. The nearer, Franciscan monastery is built directly adjacent to the restored fifth-century "white synagogue" constructed of marble, which rests on a basalt foundation that may be from the synagogue of Jesus' day. Meanwhile, the Greek Orthodox property to the northeast covers a wide area of largely unexcavated ruins. The site of a Roman Bathhouse (possibly built on the foundations of a first-century version) lies on that end of the town, probably indicating the presence of a contingent of Roman troops barracked there. The hills of the Golan are visible in the distance. Photos by the author.

Copyright © 2024 by Tony Stoltzfus
2178 Terra Nova Drive, Redding, CA. 96003
www.Coach22.com

All Rights reserved. No part of this publication may be reproduced in any form without written permission from Tony Stoltzfus.

Cover Design by Tony Stoltzfus

Unless otherwise identified, all Scripture quotations in this book are taken from *The New American Standard Bible*, Copyright © 1960, 1962, 1963, 1968, 1971, 1972, 1973, 1975, 1977, 1995 by The Lockman Foundation
Used by permission.

Photos from Unsplash, Pixabay, Deposit Photos, and the author.

Also by Tony Stoltzfus:

How to Read the Bible Like a Human Being
Questions for Jesus: Conversational Prayer Around Your Deepest Desires
The Questions for Jesus Mobile App
The Invitation: Transforming the Heart Through Desire Fulfilled
The Calling Journey: Mapping the Stages of a Leader's Life Call
Heaven's Perspective: Stories from the Book of Life
Leadership Coaching: The Disciplines, Skills and Heart of a Christian Coach
Coaching Questions: A Coach's Guide to Powerful Asking Skills
A Leader's Life Purpose Workbook
Christian Life Coaching Handbook
Peer Coach Training Facilitator's Guide
Peer Coach Training Workbook

To order bulk copies of this *Workbook*,
or other materials by Tony Stoltzfus, visit:

www.LaHB.net/store

TABLE OF CONTENTS

How to Study the Bible with the Emotional Brain 4

The Feeding of the Five Thousand 7

Walking on the Water 17

Hand Washing and Corban 27

The Syrophoenician Woman 37

Bonus Material | From the Book 46

HOW TO STUDY THE BIBLE WITH THE EMOTIONAL BRAIN

How to Read the Bible Like a Human Being is designed to revitalize and deepen your connection with scripture by studying it with the lesser-used side of your mind—the emotional brain. Using a different brain means that these studies have entirely different goals, use different tools and look for different things than most others. Let's take a quick look at what makes this approach unique.

Our goal is to experience Jesus' humanity. The emotional brain learns by *immersing itself* in a thing, so we want to visualize and experience his human life on earth. We feel the wooden mast rocking on Peter's boat, breathe the odor of fish and sweat, hear the timbers groan as it rides the waves.

But the rational brain learns by *standing outside* a thing, at an objective distance, to remove messy emotions from your thinking and focus on the facts. If your rational side is in charge of buying a car, you research the gas mileage, cost of ownership, etc. before you ever set foot on a car lot. You want to know all *about* the car so you can make a rational decision. The experience of cruising down the boulevard in a candy-apple-red ragtop while the hot girls ooh and aah is just a distraction.

The rational mind is great tool for learning good doctrine, applying the Word to daily life, and for grasping abstract concepts like grace, forgiveness or glory. But there's a hidden down-side: *the rational approach works by creating distance between you and the Jesus you study.* It's the difference between looking at the ten-thousand-foot view of a map versus actually walking the countryside, or reading a textbook about hormones versus finding the love of your life. You can't fully grasp God's love without loving him and being loved—the experience is a crucial part of understanding it. In the same way, you can't fully understand scripture without experiencing it with your emotional brain.

> **EXAMPLE: HARVESTING GRAIN ON THE SABBATH (MARK 2:23-28)**
> - To learn the rational truth in this passage, I read a commentary exploring Jesus' view of Sabbath-keeping, or find a lesson in those verses I can apply to my daily life.
> - To *experience* the passage with the emotional brain, I get some heads of wheat, rub them between my palms and eat some of the wheat berries to see what it was like.

A DIFFERENT PROCESS

While the rational brain gets its information through words, facts and concepts, the emotional brain understands through *image, experience and metaphor.* One way to grasp Jesus or Peter or John with your emotional brain is to put yourself in their shoes and experience what they did. So pop those wheat berries in your mouth—and chew, and chew, and *chew* those gummy little beads! You'll probably come away thinking, "I'd have to be *really* hungry to scavenge a meal like this!" And then you wonder, "How often were the disciples hungry? What was their everyday life really like?" Now you are thinking with your emotional brain.

THREE KEY TOOLS
- **Visualize** the scene.
- **Feel** what they feel.
- **Identify** with their experience.

Sometimes we can replicate a first-century Israelite's experience, but more often we recreate it through *Visualization*. That's the first of the three key tools for emotional-brain study. Picture Jesus walking the narrow alleys of Capernaum, with ten-foot-high, black stone walls on either hand. Or imagine the smells as he wakes in Peter's house after sleeping in his clothes in a room with twelve other guys! I you can *see* a scene, you can *feel* it, and if you feel it, you can *identify* with it.

Our second tool is experiencing the *Emotions* in the pictures we make. For example, Jairus recruits Jesus to deal with the emergency of his dying daughter (see Mark 5:22-35), but Jesus gets distracted along the way—and the girl dies! How would he feel? How would YOU feel if you were Jairus? People in Jesus' day had the same emotions we do, so the gateway to understanding their emotions is asking what we'd feel if we were in that situation (after correcting for cultural differences).

Doing the work to build a rich, emotion-filled picture of the story triggers connections between Jairus' experiences and our own. That's called *Identification*, our third tool. We remember times when we've gotten delayed on the way to something important, and feel the sinking dread in our gut that goes with it. When we can connect our own memories with the experience of a bible character, we truly understand, with our hearts as well as our heads. This is what learning with the emotional brain feels like—that instinctive sense that you 'get' someone. And that's what we're going for!

> **Example:** in the shortest verse in the bible, where "Jesus wept" over Lazarus' death (John 11:35), a rational bible study might ask:
> - *Doctrinal questions:* What quality of God do Jesus' tears reveal?
> - *Behavioral questions:* How is my heart broken for those who are suffering in my city?
>
> An emotional brain study might ask:
> - *Visualization questions:* Picture Jesus' tears running down his cheeks. Where do they fall?
> - *Emotion questions:* What is going on in Jesus' heart at that moment?
> - *Identification questions:* When in your life did someone you loved die unexpectedly? What did that feel like? How was Jesus' experience with Lazarus like yours?

A DIFFERENT LEARNING METHOD

These studies use an interactive *Discovery Learning* method, where group leaders ask questions to help participants come up with their own insights. Adults remember up to **ten times** as much when they discuss something versus being lectured. So, there is NO teaching in these studies! Everyone participates, everyone learns, everyone shares. Since we are using our own life experience to understand biblical characters, anyone who has life experiences (that's all of us!) has something valuable to contribute, from brand new believers to those who've studied scripture for decades.

WRITING NARRATIVES

The cherry on the top of each study comes in week three. Each participant picks a character from the bible story, and writes a *Visual Narrative* of what happened from that person's perspective. We use a technique called *Free Writing* that bypasses all the onerous stuff you had to endure in high school English: no spell-checking, no editing or rewriting, and no grammar-nazi stuff. You just write—it's fun! Reading narratives to each other offers amazing insights into the passage and builds a surprising intimacy in the group. To produce a great narrative, you have to write out of your own experience. So each narrative tells us something about both the story in the bible and *your* life story!

Participants consistently report that writing and sharing narratives is where it all comes together for them—that the characters come alive in a way that changes how they look at scripture forever.

These studies rely heavily on using our imaginations to fill in the missing details in the oh-so-short stories we have in the gospels. We encourage making up details to bring your narratives to life! The key to making this work is that we are NOT making doctrine! That's a task for rational study—in fact, we test our emotional-brain insights against what we know of sound, rational doctrine.

> **EXAMPLE: THE WOMAN WITH THE ISSUE OF BLOOD**
> She was literally shaking with fear when she was found out. A good modern analogy is that she was having a panic attack. If someone in the group has had one, we can use that to fill in the missing details of how she felt and what she experienced, all while still holding the idea lightly. The goal is to feel what she felt, not create a new theology of panic attacks!

How to Read the Bible Like a Human Being | Mark Book Six

THE FEEDING OF THE FIVE THOUSAND
MARK 6:33-44

BREAD VENDOR IN JERUSALEM

PASSAGE: MARK 6:33-44 (NASB)

³¹And He said to them, "Come away by yourselves to a secluded place and rest a while." (For there were many people coming and going, and they did not even have time to eat.) ³²They went away in the boat to a secluded place by themselves.

³³The people saw them going, and many recognized them and ran there together on foot from all the cities, and got there ahead of them. ³⁴When Jesus went ashore, He saw a large crowd, and He felt compassion for them because they were like sheep without a shepherd; and He began to teach them many things.

³⁵When it was already quite late, His disciples came to Him and said, "This place is desolate and it is already quite late; ³⁶send them away so that they may go into the surrounding countryside and villages and buy themselves something to eat."

³⁷But He answered them, "You give them something to eat!"

And they said to Him, "Shall we go and spend 200 denarii on bread and give them something to eat?"

³⁸And He said to them, "How many loaves do you have? Go look!" And when they found out, they said, "Five, and two fish."

³⁹And He commanded them all to sit down by groups on the green grass. ⁴⁰They sat down in groups of hundreds and of fifties. ⁴¹And He took the five loaves and the two fish, and looking up toward heaven, He blessed the food and broke the loaves and He kept giving them to the disciples to set before them; and He divided up the two fish among them all. ⁴²They all ate and were satisfied, ⁴³and they picked up twelve full baskets of the broken pieces, and also of the fish. ⁴⁴There were five thousand men who ate the loaves.

BACKGROUND INFO
THE CROWD SIZE AND WOMEN OUTSIDE THE HOME

If you were told that a big crowd went out to the park Saturday—5000 men attended, plus all the women and children—how many total people were there? Westerners would assume as many women as men, plus children, so we might calculate 15,000 people. But if it happened two millennia ago in a different culture, we'll have to use different assumptions.

In the Galilee of Jesus' day, for every adult man there would have been five or six women and children. But it is highly unlikely that that many came. Mothers with small children couldn't just take off for a two-mile jaunt across the countryside. Rabbinic literature of the time also tells us that due to concerns about sexual impurity, women (at least in wealthy households) were expected to stay largely in the house. As in, quarantined there:

> *"While a man's primary responsibility was seen as public, a woman's life was confined almost entirely within the private family sphere… In Talmudic times, respectable women were expected to stay within the confines of the home. The terminology for a prostitute was "one who goes abroad."*[1]

> *"It is the way of a woman to stay at home and it is the way of a man to go out into the marketplace"* (Bereshit Rabbah 18:1; cf. Taanit 23b).

> *"I was a pure maiden and left not my father's house…"* 4 Maccabees 18:7 (AD 35)

We see these cultural expectations in the astonishment of the disciples that Jesus would talk with the Samaritan woman at the well. Alone! It just wasn't done!

---

[1] https://jewsforjesus.org/learn/the-role-of-women-in-the-bible

While believing that women *should* be secluded in the home, the sages recognized it was not practical for everyone. Poor women (i.e. the vast majority of women) needed to work in the fields, and had no slaves to run their outside errands. But there was probably still considerable social pressure for women to minimize time away from home.

Another belief that limited women from attending is their relative level of education. Three is some evidence girls participated in the early years of school in Jesus' day, over the following centuries they were gradually excluded, with caustic reasoning like this:

"It would be better to burn the words of the law than teach them to women," said Rabbi Eliezer.

"Based on the passage in Deuteronomy 4:9, "teach them to thy sons," the rabbis declared women to be exempt from the commandment to learn the Law of Moses. Indeed, the Talmud says, "It is foolishness to teach Torah to your daughter" (Sotah 20a).[2]

Therefore, my guess would be that men considerably outnumbered women, and children as well. So, the total crowd might be less than 10,000—maybe a lot less.

Understanding the culture of Jesus' day only increases my awe at how he empowered women. In a culture where women weren't even *allowed in church* (i.e. in the inner courts of the temple where actual sacrifices took place), Jesus spoke to women alone, traveled with women disciples, taught women, drew his financial support from women, pointed out women as examples of good behavior, etc. Jesus was incredibly radical for his day.

BREAD

In *What Did The Ancient Israelites Eat?* author Nathan MacDonald relates that "breads contributed between fifty to seventy-five per cent of overall calories: far in excess of modern diets." And, "Meat was incredibly valuable. At the time of the Persian Empire, a sheep was equivalent to three months' [rations of] wheat." Food was a large expense for the poor, soaking up as much as half their entire income (another thirty percent might have gone to taxes). So other than fish, the average Galilean might have only eaten meat occasionally as part of a feast. This limited diet (they weren't into vegetables in those days) led to an array of health problems. Probably half the population suffered from malnutrition at any given time. And since the flour they baked with was hand-ground in stone mills, the grit was very hard on their teeth, too.

The poor baked bread once a week (since fuel was hard to come by, dung was used), and set their loaves out in the sun to dry so they would keep, which is why they often dipped their bread in a sauce or stew when eating it. A wife with a family of five or six could spend three hours a day just milling the flour for baking. (Think of the biceps on those women!) One common type of bread was a flatbread baked by literally sticking dough to the sides of a hot clay oven. Another type of loaf was about the size of our dinner rolls.

A family meal in those times began with the father breaking the bread, blessing it and handing it out, just as Jesus did in the feeding miracles and at the last supper.

A first-century table. A domed oven is in the rear.

---

[2] https://jewsforjesus.org/learn/the-role-of-women-in-the-bible

DO THE MATH: HOW MUCH FOOD WAS THAT?

It's a fun exercise to try to calculate how much bread and fish it would have taken to feed the crowd. Try starting here:

- They ate two main meals plus a snack for breakfast at that time. So, assume Jesus served up an 800-calorie meal (figuring a 2000-calorie-a-day diet).
- Bread is about 1200 calories a pound, while dried fish is 1700 calories a pound.
- Assume bread was sixty percent of the calories in their diet (i.e. 480 calories in this meal).

480 calories of bread weighs 0.4 pounds, plus 320 calories of fish (0.2 pounds) totals 0.6 pounds of food per person. Multiply that by 7,000 people, and you get two **tons** of food!

We can check our work by calculating in a different way. There were two wave offerings set aside from all food for the priests, a 50th and a 100th (three percent total). This rule was strictly followed at the time, even by impious Jews (the penalty in Torah for misusing the wave offering was death).

Apparently, the crowd that day was unsure if the proper offerings had been taken out of the five loaves and two fish Jesus multiplied. For this 'dubiously tithed food', the Pharisees had ruled that you should break off a fragment representing that three percent of your meal and set it aside for the priests. That three percent could very well be where the twelve basketfuls of 'broken pieces' that were left over came from! The disciples carefully collected these pieces, because as food dedicated to the priests, they had to either be given to a priest or destroyed.

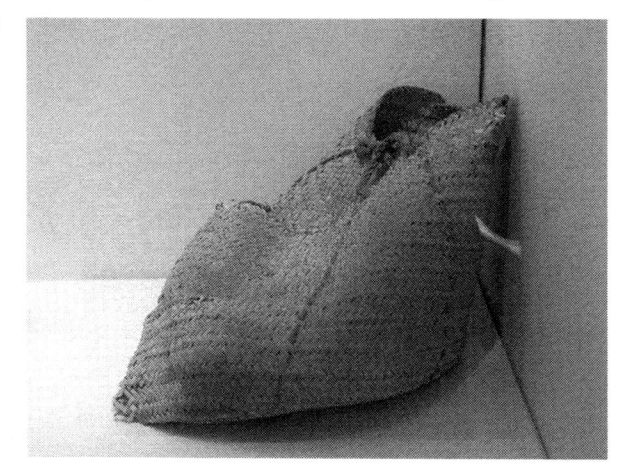

Perfectly-preserved basket from the Cave of Letters, AD 132

So, if three percent of the food Jesus made that day filled twelve full baskets, the total amount of food he created would be thirty-three times that. Twelve times thirty-three equals 396 baskets full! Now we can compare our two calculations, one yielding about 400 baskets and the other 4000 pounds, to see if they match up. If the amount of food per basket (4000 divided by 400 baskets equals ten pounds per basket) seems reasonable, our confidence that we're on the right track goes up!

DO THE MATH QUESTIONS

1. How much could a disciple carry in one trip to hand it out (hint: bread is bulky)?
2. How many trips back and forth would it take the twelve disciples to feed everyone?
3. How many disciple-loads of food would it take to satisfy each group of fifty or 100?
4. How long might it take to feed the whole crowd? What time of day might it have been by the time they were finished?

SECTION I: A VACATION RUINED

Who all was there?

When did it happen? (Time of day/year)

Where did it happen?

    Coming from/going to?

What happened before/after?

Weather

HOW DO YOU FEEL WHEN YOUR PLANS GO AWRY?

DESCRIBE WHAT IT LOOKS LIKE WHEN PEOPLE ARE RUNNING AHEAD OF THE BOAT.

WHAT DOES IT TELL YOU ABOUT JESUS THAT HIS PLANNED GETAWAY DIDN'T WORK OUT?

HEAR

SEE

TOUCH

SMELL

TASTE

SECTION II: MANAGING A HUNGRY MOB

PAINT A VISUAL PICTURE OF THIS CONVERSATION.

Sad — Grieved, Discouraged, Disappointed
Joyful — Satisfied, Grateful, Happy
Disconnected — Indifferent, Withdrawn, Shut Down
Excited — Thrilled, Passionate, Fascinated
Angry — Enraged, Disgusted, Frustrated
Peaceful — Fulfilled, Content, Calm
Inadequate — Vulnerable, Powerless, Confused
Powerful — Free, Capable, Confident
Wrong — Guilty, Broken, Ashamed
Approved — Respected, Valuable, Good
Hurt — Heart-broken, Devastated, Wronged
Safe — Secure, Protected, Comforted
Afraid — Anxious, Terrified, Threatened
Hopeful — Encouraged, Optimistic, Eager
Unloved — Rejected, Unknown, Worthless
Loved — Pursued, Cherished, Connected

© Tony Stoltzfus — www.LikeAHumanBeing.com

WHY ARE THE DISCIPLES ASKING JESUS TO SEND THE CROWD AWAY?

WHO WAS IN CHARGE OF PROCURING FOOD FOR JESUS AND HIS TEAM?

WHY DID JESUS GIVE THE DISCIPLES A CHANCE TO FEED THE CROWD?

SECTION III: THE MULTIPLICATION

WHAT VISUAL CLUES DO YOU SEE IN THESE VERSES?

HUMAN QUESTIONS

HOW WOULD I HAVE FELT?

WHY DID THEY DO THAT?

WHAT WOULD A HUMAN BEING DO?

IF I WERE IN THEIR SHOES...

WHAT QUESTIONS DOES THE LOGISTICS OF FEEDING 5,000 PEOPLE RAISE?

WHERE EXACTLY DID THE BREAD MULTIPLY?

DO THE MATH: HOW LONG DID IT TAKE TO FEED EVERYONE?

QUESTIONS FOR JESUS

1. Jesus, when you got in the boat, what were you looking forward to on a day off?

2. Jesus, what does compassion feel like to you?

3. Jesus, when your boys asked to send the crowd away, what did you love in them?

4. Jesus, what was in your heart as you watched all those people eating?

ADDITIONAL RESOURCES
NOTE: Live links for these resources are on-line at: LaHB.net/mark633

WOMEN'S ROLES
"…these attitudes naturally went alongside an attitude that it was improper for a woman to talk to a man."
Man and Woman in Biblical Perspective by James Hurley, pg. 65.

"Teaching women was a waste of time, they said. 'It would be better to burn the words of the law than teach them to women,' said Rabbi Eliezer."
https://escapetoreality.org/2020/07/09/jesus-pioneer-of-womens-education/

"Drawing on the work of sociologists, Megan McKenna suggests in her book Not Counting Women and Children (Orbis, 1994) that the ratio of women and children to adult men would be 5 to 1 or 6 to 1…"
https://reformedjournal.com/not-counting-women-children/

BREAD
"You can expect to pay up to half a denarius a day just to feed yourself."
https://www.katrinadhamel.com/post/wages-food-prices-and-shopping-for-the-family-in-first-century-israel

"Four modii of wheat could feed a slave for a month, assuming he only ate bread."
https://sites.google.com/a/saintmarksschool.org/grade7rome/roman-money/what-can-i-buy-with-a-denarius

"In Palestine specifically, wheat prices were significantly cheaper, up to one-third the cost of wheat in Rome. Hence, a family of four in Palestine may have been able to survive on as little as 70 denarii a year." (LDS source)
https://journal.interpreterfoundation.org/was-the-denarius-a-daily-wage-a-note-on-the-parable-of-the-two-debtors-in-luke-740-43/

"The crowds of 5,000 and 4,000 who ate the miraculous five loaves and seven loaves treated the food as doubtful, and therefore left twelve and seven baskets of broken-off fragments…it is likely that these fragments were the elevation offering…"
Traditions of the Rabbis from the Era of the New Testament, by David Instone-Brewer, page 182.

BLESSING BREAD
"These are the normal actions of the Jewish head of the family at a meal, taking bread, pronouncing the blessing, breaking it, and distributing it…the formula of blessing, which for bread took the traditional form 'Blessed art thou, Lord our God, King of the world, who bringest forth bread from the earth'" (Mishnah Ber. 6:1) – NIGTC

BASKETS
"A kophinos, was 'a wicker basket,' (made of twigs or branches) … that could be carried on the back to hold provisions, it is believed that they were Ephah size, about 3/5 bushel, (like a knapsack size.)"
http://www.barr-family.com/godsword/baskets.htm

"Kophinos were common containers on farms, and they seem to have been very strong, since they were imagined as appropriate for hoisting stones or for lowering men…" A History of Trust in Ancient Greece, by Steven Johnstone
https://books.google.com/books?id=r5TvmDaNWRoC&pg=PA44&lpg=PA44&dq=basket+kophinos+first+century

How to Read the Bible Like a Human Being | Mark Book Six

WALKING ON THE WATER
MARK 6:45-52

VIEW FROM THE EREMOS CAVE

PASSAGE: MARK 6:45-52 (NASB)
(See also Matthew 14:22-33: John 6:15-21)

⁴⁵Immediately Jesus made His disciples get into the boat and go ahead of Him to the other side to Bethsaida, while He Himself was sending the crowd away. ⁴⁶After bidding them farewell, He left for the mountain to pray.

⁴⁷When it was evening, the boat was in the middle of the sea, and He was alone on the land. ⁴⁸Seeing them straining at the oars, for the wind was against them, at about the fourth watch of the night He came to them, walking on the sea; and He intended to pass by them.

⁴⁹But when they saw Him walking on the sea, they supposed that it was a ghost, and cried out; ⁵⁰for they all saw Him and were terrified. But immediately He spoke with them and said to them, "Take courage; it is I, do not be afraid." ⁵¹Then He got into the boat with them, and the wind stopped; and they were utterly astonished, ⁵²for they had not gained any insight from the incident of the loaves, but their heart was hardened.

JOHN 6:15-21

¹⁵So Jesus, perceiving that they were intending to come and take Him by force to make Him king, withdrew again to the mountain by Himself alone.

¹⁶Now when evening came, His disciples went down to the sea, ¹⁷and after getting into a boat, they started to cross the sea to Capernaum. It had already become dark, and Jesus had not yet come to them. ¹⁸The sea began to be stirred up because a strong wind was blowing. ¹⁹Then, when they had rowed about three or four miles, they saw Jesus walking on the sea and drawing near to the boat; and they were frightened.

²⁰But He said to them, "It is I; do not be afraid." ²¹So they were willing to receive Him into the boat, and immediately the boat was at the land to which they were going.

BACKGROUND INFO
SEA OF GALILEE WEATHER

The weather on lake Kinneret is unusual because of the lake's unusual location, at over 600 feet below sea level. It rests in a bowl, with mountains 3000 feet above the lake on the east. In summer, Mediterranean Sea breezes out of the west are accelerated as they drop into the bowl, with the wind often kicking up in the afternoon and calming after dark. Most summer days experience winds of twenty miles per hour and more at some point during the day under clear skies.

The Sea of Galilee is only eight miles wide and thirteen miles long. (In this photo you are looking across the width of the lake from Tiberius to the east.) The lake's small size limits the size of the waves that can form in it. The 'fetch' is the distance wind travels across the water stirring up waves. On the Pacific Ocean, this can be thousands of miles. For the disciples in the boat, it was only five to seven miles at the absolute maximum.

The Sea of Galilee, seen at sunrise from Tiberias.

However, their boat had a low freeboard (the distance from the top of the sides down to the water) of only two or three feet, and it was quite heavily loaded with a dozen men on board, so it wouldn't have taken huge waves to cause problems.

While summer is dominated by ocean winds out of the west, winter weather is more variable. Sudden storms are caused when cooler air from the mountains on the east drops rapidly into the subtropical climate around the lake. That is probably what happened here. In the feeding of the five thousand story immediately before this passage, Jesus had people sit down "on the green grass." The grass in Galilee turns brown by May. Therefore, events in this passage likely took place in the spring.

The worst storms are caused by the 'whistler' winds out of the east, occasionally producing waves that damage buildings and boats on the western shore. The disciples apparently were rowing into the teeth of one of these eastern storms.

I saw evidence of how powerful they can be in May of 2022 while walking down the deserted Tiberias waterfront. All the shops were closed, and I wondered if they'd all gone out of business because of Covid. Normally this area hosted over a million people a year! Stepping through the torn-up concrete and rubble of one building, its windows broken or boarded over, I speculated that it was being torn down (see photo).

What I didn't know is that a 'whistler' storm only a week before we arrived had sent waves crashing over the seawall and flooding dozens of shops and restaurants on the Tiberias promenade. With winds up to 87 mph, the storm caused 50 million dollars in damages!

THE JESUS BOAT

As they left the small harbor at the Seven Springs (Tabgha), what kind of boat did Jesus' disciples travel in? It was likely a vessel belonging to the Peter/Andrew/Zebedee brothers fishing syndicate (Luke 5:10). The Romans sold fishing concessions on the lake, so fishermen had to band together in these collectives to afford to fish. Before modern technology came to the lake, the largest traditional wooden fishing boats were in the twenty-five-to-thirty-foot range. Given that the boat in scripture regularly traveled with thirteen men aboard, it was probably about that size.

Amazingly, we now have a first-century example: the so-called "Jesus Boat" displayed at Ginosaur near where it was found. The ship was discovered poking out of the mud of the lake bottom at a time when the water was at a historically low level. This boat was roughly twenty-seven feet long and seven-and-a-half feet wide, with a shallow draft, a single, square sail and a crew of five: four rowers and a helmsman. She was built 'shell-first' of mortise and tenon construction joining short and often narrow planks. The ribs on the inside of the hull were crooked

The restored Jesus Boat, showing her rough interior

branches formed to the curve of the planks. It was an old boat, that had been repaired many times and finally stripped for parts before being sunk in the lake after as much as a century of use. It was built a few decades before Jesus' birth out of ten different species of wood, showing either that good timber was in short supply, or that it was just too expensive for this type of vessel. The boatwright was skilled—he just had to work with inferior material.

The wide 'deck' at the stern is where large nets like the seine were stowed on the way to and from the fishing grounds. Paddles near the stern are steering oars used by the helmsman (Peter?) to direct their course. Forward of this is the single mast. The four oarsmen sat two on the edge of the front deck and two on the crossbeam that supported the mast, facing rearward. Unlike the pristine model shown here, her outsides would have been covered in black pitch to protect the timbers from rotting, while her insides were darkened and slimed from exposure to water, nets and fish.

The simple rigging on the boat explains some of the details in this story. Technically, it had a single, loose-footed, brailed square sail. Loose-footed means there was no spar or yard at the bottom of the sail—it hung loose. The sail was furled (or drawn upward to stow it) sort of like a venetian blind, with ropes called brails passing through metal rings in the edges of the sail. Pulling on these brails bunched the sail together at the upper yard in accordion-folds.

A reconstructed model of the Jesus Boat. At the rear are two steering oars set at an angle: note the tiller bars at the top.

The implication of all this is that the ship could not sail into the wind.[3] In fact, researchers of ancient voyages have concluded that reasonable sailors would not even *attempt* to take longer journeys upwind, because of limits of these sails and the navigational constraints of the time. So, when the wind rose that night blowing toward them from the eastern mountains, the sail was useless. The only option the disciples had was to row straight into it—or turn back. So why did they keep going forward all night, making little or no headway? Well, fully-loaded with a dozen men, including half-a-dozen landlubbers who might do something stupid at the worst possible moment, the fishermen would have been loath to turn the ship broadside to the waves, lest they capsize. So, the men may have been forced to keep going forward.

---

[3] See https://www.tandfonline.com/doi/full/10.1080/10572414.2023.2186688, a scientific paper on the capabilities of mariners using this type of craft.

SECTION I: THE DISCIPLES LEAVE, JESUS PRAYS | VS. 45-46

VISUAL CUES
Who all was there? _____

When did it happen? (Time of day/year) _____

Where did it happen? _____

   Coming from/going to? _____

What happened before/after? _____

Weather _____

WALK WITH JESUS AS HE WENT UP THE MOUNTAIN TO PRAY...
_____
_____
_____
_____

WHAT ARE THE DISCIPLES THINKING WILL HAPPEN?
_____
_____
_____
_____

WHAT'S GOING ON IN THE HEARTS OF JESUS AND HIS DISCIPLES?
_____
_____
_____
_____

HEAR

SEE

TOUCH

SMELL

TASTE

SECTION II — WALKING ON WATER | VS. 47-48

IT'S THE FOURTH WATCH OF THE NIGHT: WHAT'S GOING ON IN THE BOAT?

Sad	Joyful
Grieved	Satisfied
Discouraged	Grateful
Disappointed	Happy
Disconnected	**Excited**
Indifferent	Thrilled
Withdrawn	Passionate
Shut Down	Fascinated
Angry	**Peaceful**
Enraged	Fulfilled
Disgusted	Content
Frustrated	Calm
Inadequate	**Powerful**
Vulnerable	Free
Powerless	Capable
Confused	Confident
Wrong	**Approved**
Guilty	Respected
Broken	Valuable
Ashamed	Good
Hurt	**Safe**
Heart-broken	Secure
Devastated	Protected
Wronged	Comforted
Afraid	**Hopeful**
Anxious	Encouraged
Terrified	Optimistic
Threatened	Eager
Unloved	**Loved**
Rejected	Pursued
Unknown	Cherished
Worthless	Connected

© Tony Stoltzfus — www.LikeAHumanBeing.com

HOW COULD JESUS TELL THAT HIS BOYS WERE IN TROUBLE?

WHAT WOULD IT BE LIKE TO WALK ON WATER?

SECTION III: SEEING A GHOST | VS. 49-52

WHERE ARE THE DIFFERENT PEOPLE SITTING IN THE BOAT?

HUMAN QUESTIONS

HOW WOULD I HAVE FELT?

WHY DID THEY DO THAT?

WHAT DOES IT TELL YOU ABOUT THEIR EMOTIONAL STATE THAT THEY SAW A GHOST?

WHAT WOULD A HUMAN BEING DO?

IF I WERE IN THEIR SHOES...

WHEN HAVE YOU SAID, "IT'S OKAY, IT'S ME!"

PICTURE THE SCENE AS JESUS STEPS INTO THE BOAT...

QUESTIONS FOR JESUS

1. Jesus, what were you feeling when you heard about John's death?

2. Jesus, what did you like about praying in that little cave?

3. Jesus, what were you experiencing when you walked on the water?

4. Jesus, when the disciples thought you were a ghost—how did that strike you?

ADDITIONAL RESOURCES
NOTE: Live links to these resources are on-line at: LaHB.net/mark645

SEA OF GALILEE WEATHER
"[On] May 15, strong easterly winds blew in the north of the country…of about 80 km/h with gusts close to 140 km/h [87mph] causing trees to collapse and block roadways…" https://www.israeltoday.co.il/read/bible-level-wind-storm-batters-sea-of-galilee/

"67% of the storms start between 10:00 am and 4:00 pm, have a duration of 4 to 12 hours and an average wind speed of 7.6-10.0 meters per second (17-22 mph)." http://www.magniel.com/hmtj/papers/vks83/vks.html

"Lower Galilee, where Jesus lived most of his life, was Israel's lushest region, known for its sunny, temperate climate and its spring-watered lands." http://blog.adw.org/2014/07/what-was-the-climate-and-weather-of-israel-like-at-the-time-of-jesus/

"From approximately February to April…the Holy Land is carpeted in wildflowers." https://www.botanic.co.il/wp-content/uploads/2017/09/The-Wildflowers-of-Israel-lr.pdf

THE 'JESUS BOAT'
"Constructed primarily of cedar planks joined together by pegged mortise and tenon joints and nails, the boat is shallow drafted with a flat bottom, allowing it to get very close to the shore while fishing." https://madainproject.com/boat_of_jesus

"Obviously, the Boatwright had made do with timbers that normally would have been discarded in a Mediterranean boatyard. This indicates an extreme wood shortage in which every possible scrap of wood was used in the boat-building process." https://www.jesusboat.com/jesusboat-archive/ancient-seafaring-and-the-jesus-boat/

"If the vessel's hand-me-down hull is any indication, the boat's sail was also likely to have been of a dingy, oft-repaired patchwork design…" https://www.academia.edu/4595079/The_Sea_of_Galilee_Boat

BOATS IN A STORM
"… I encountered swirling gale-force winds and waves coming at me from all directions. As my fear increased, my grip on the oars grew tighter. I was tiring quickly and my hands, forearms, and back ached." https://smallboatsmonthly.com/article/rowing-rough-water/

"We could not stay as we were—we would be blown over, and we could never right the boat in such conditions. Night was coming, and if we capsized we would not survive." https://www.yachtingworld.com/voyages/storm-sailing-16ft-open-boat-extract-sea-takes-no-prisoners-peter-clutterbuck-128269

HOW DID JESUS SEE THE BOAT?
"Rod cells [in our eyes] are seriously sensitive, able to detect a single photon of light, but they lack the ability to see color and detail. On a moonless night away from city lights, the nightscape is painted in shades of gray..." https://skyandtelescope.org/astronomy-blogs/struck-moonlight12312014/

"…on black nights, the horizon immediately in front of your eyes is actually not seen… This fact is very little appreciated by civilians, but it is one of the most important facts to an expert lookout searching at night."
1943 Navy Lookout Manual. https://www.history.navy.mil/research/library/online-reading-room/title-list-alphabetically/l/lookout-manual-1943.html

How to Read the Bible Like a Human Being | Mark Book Six

HAND WASHING AND CORBAN
MARK 7:1-13

PASSAGE: MARK 7:1-13 (NASB)
(See also Matthew 15:1-9)

¹The Pharisees and some of the scribes gathered around Him when they had come from Jerusalem, ²and had seen that some of His disciples were eating their bread with impure hands, that is, unwashed. ³(For the Pharisees and all the Jews do not eat unless they carefully wash their hands, thus observing the traditions of the elders; ⁴and when they come from the marketplace, they do not eat unless they cleanse themselves; and there are many other things which they have received in order to observe, such as the washing of cups and pitchers and copper pots.)

⁵The Pharisees and the scribes asked Him, "Why do Your disciples not walk according to the tradition of the elders, but eat their bread with impure hands?"

⁶And He said to them, "Rightly did Isaiah prophesy of you hypocrites, as it is written: 'This people honors me with their lips, but their heart is far away from me. ⁷But in vain do they worship me, teaching as doctrines the precepts of men.' ⁸Neglecting the commandment of God, you hold to the tradition of men."

⁹He was also saying to them, "You are experts at setting aside the commandment of God in order to keep your tradition. ¹⁰For Moses said, 'Honor your father and your mother'; and, 'He who speaks evil of father or mother, is to be put to death'; ¹¹but you say, 'If a man says to his father or his mother, whatever I have that would help you is Corban (that is to say, given to God),' ¹²you no longer permit him to do anything for his father or his mother; ¹³thus invalidating the word of God by your tradition which you have handed down; and you do many things such as that.

BACKGROUND INFO
THE WRITTEN AND THE ORAL LAW

Through Jewish eyes, the Tanakh (our Old Testament) is composed of three sections:

1. The Law (The five books of Moses)
2. The Prophets (Joshua, Judges, Samuel, Kings, Isaiah, Jeremiah, etc.)
3. The Writings (Everything else: Psalms, Proverbs, Job, etc.)

The heart of the Judaism is the five books of the law: Torah. The Pharisees held that these laws needed inspired interpretation to be properly applied. They came to believe that their 'Oral Law' was given by God to Moses, who passed it on to the seventy elders, who then transmitted it through the generations in an unbroken chain down to Jesus' day. These traditional interpretations, memorized and expanded upon over the years, were later written down as the Mishna. Because of this connection to Moses' authority, the Pharisees held that the Oral Law (as well as Torah) was legally binding, though the Sadducees and Essenes disagreed.

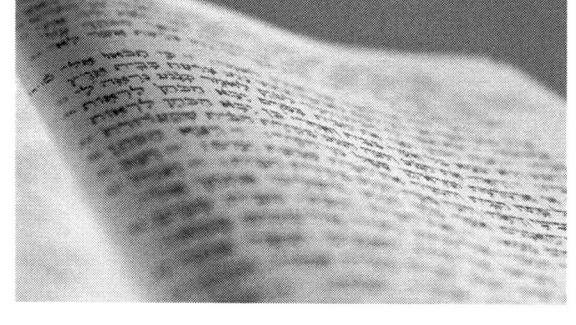

However, different Pharisaic teachers held to slightly different interpretations of these rules. And while claiming they originated with Moses, they felt free to add to and alter them as new situations arose that required a ruling.

Jesus insists that Torah is divine in Mark 5:17: "Do not think that I came to abolish the Law or the Prophets; I did not come to abolish but to fulfill" ('to abolish' is a technical term meaning 'to wrongly interpret', while 'fulfill' means to 'correctly interpret'). But on different occasions he ignores the Pharisaic oral code on harvesting and threshing on the Sabbath (see Mark 2:24), ritual washing before eating, purity rules (he touches the unclean while healing), and others. He is *very* critical when Pharisaic rulings directly contradict Torah, as with the Corban issue (see below). But on other occasions, such as when he healed the man with the withered hand (see Mark 3:5), he takes meticulous care to follow these rules. In that situation he had the man stretch out his own hand instead of stretching it out for him, which the Pharisees would have viewed as illegal.

Overall, Jesus seemed to feel that the problem with the Oral Law was one of focus. To him, purity of heart was the goal, not outward ritual purity. Yet the oral code put so much emphasis on ever-more-specific rules (Torah has 80,000 words, but the Oral Law recorded in the Babylonian Talmud has 1.9 million!)[4] that he felt the Pharisees were 'straining out a gnat[5] and swallowing a camel'. Instead, Jesus taught a very simple rule of life, or *halakh*: love God and each other!

In the New Testament church, the indwelling Spirit is the provider of inspired interpretation, replacing the oral traditions of the elders with a living relationship with the Spirit. The Pharisees expanded and interpreted the oral code to fit new situations, and similarly the church felt free to make new rulings (for instance, that Gentile converts did not need to become Jews to be Christians) at the prompting of the Spirit.

ALLUDING TO THE BROADER CONTEXT

Since the scribes and Pharisees had memorized the entire Tanakh, just alluding to a verse would bring up the whole larger context in the hearer's mind. This was a common technique in rabbinic discourse, so it is important to look at the quote in context to see what else Jesus might be saying. He refers to Isaiah 29:13, so I've paraphrased verses nine to sixteen here:

> *It's like you're drunk! God has poured spiritual blindness out on all of you sages. So, my teaching is beyond you. It's like a book in a foreign language you can't read. The people ask you what to make of me, but you have no clue. You are failed shepherds, unable to fulfill your most basic functions. That's because your reverence is mere rule-following—you don't actually know God at all.*
>
> *Therefore, God is bypassing you to do great things with the people—through me! You'll have no part in it. The wisdom you "wise men" judge me with will perish. You've taken secret, evil counsel together to undermine me and my teaching, because you think no one—even God!—will discern your impure motive to condemn me. You've got it backwards! God made you, yet you have the gall to tell him what he can and can't do!*

CORBAN

Corban is a Hebrew word meaning 'gift' or 'offering'. In the Old Testament it is used on eighty occasions to refer to a dedicated offering brought to the temple in Jerusalem. One possibility is that Jesus is using 'Corban' here in this sense (of a gift *actually given* to the temple). However, by Jesus' time the word had taken on a second meaning: "that which has been set aside as a gift to be given later to God, but which is still at the disposal of the owner" (Louw-Nida). It was essentially a legal device that allowed the person to keep the property in his possession and even benefit from its use, all while innocently claiming it couldn't be used to, say, pay off a debt or support one's parents, because it was dedicated to God.

A present-day analogy might be someone placing his assets into a shell company owned by his mother before

The Israel Museum model of the temple mount of Jesus' day. The temple is in the center; the Royal Stoa is to the left.

---

[4] https://www.talmudology.com/jeremybrownmdgmailcom/2019/12/30/berachot-2-how-many-words-are-in-the-babylonian-talmud

[5] Jesus is referring to something practiced in his day: straining a drink through a piece of cloth to keep from ingesting an unclean insect. Gnats were the smallest unclean animal, and camels the largest.

declaring bankruptcy, to keep the court from taking them away. He no longer 'owns' these assets in the legal sense, though everybody knows they are still his. Origen, one of the early church fathers, refers to this practice:

> *"There existed a method of spiteful revenge on debtors who possessed the means to repay their loans but refused to do so: the creditors would declare that the money owed was korban—a gift to the poor. The money was now owed to God, and while the creditor would not be repaid, he had the satisfaction of knowing that the debtor had not escaped scot free. This system, Origen argued, was transferred by the Pharisees to the realm of support owed parents by their children. A child could shirk his obligation to support his parents by declaring that the money was now korban. … As in the case of the creditor above, the child could not keep the money himself; no savings to him resulted, since the money had to go to the Temple. The child's only benefit was spite."* [6]

(A brief digression: we live in a society with separation of church and state, so when the Bible says something is a 'law' we tend to hear it as 'spiritual law'—an ethos we choose to follow but which is not legally binding in court. But for the Jews of Jesus day, the Torah and the Oral Law were *also the governmental law*. Local disputes on questions like this were judged before a scribe in court by Jewish law. So, this is a legal question and not just an ethical one!)

There was a third way the word 'Corban' came to be used that stretched the original meaning almost beyond recognition. Because it was a vow to God, the scribes ruled that adding the word 'Corban' to any vow you made about anything *gave that vow the same legal weight as a vow to dedicate something to God.*[7]

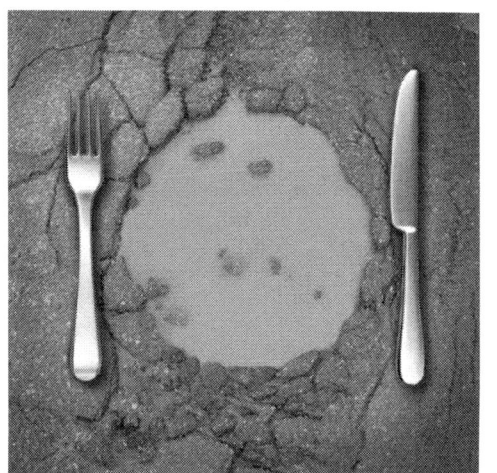

Lois Tverberg says,[8] "This seems to have been a common way of venting your disgust in ancient times. People would explode with, '*Corban* what I would eat with you!' or '*Corban* be my legs that would walk with you!' '*Corban* be my mouth that speaks with you!' The person was, in effect, vowing before God not to eat or walk or speak with someone else."

Jesus' hearers likely understood his example in this third sense. The son had vowed something like, "Corban if I support you in your old age!" He hadn't dedicated his resources to God, so they were his to use how he pleased. But because he used the magic word 'Corban', the vow was legally binding. Even though the obligation to support his parents was enshrined in the Ten Commandments, he had a scribal get-out-of-jail-free card that absolved him of any need to obey it![9] And if he ever regretted his rash vow and wanted to repent, the scribes had ruled in court that he was legally bound to keep it.

---

[6] https://janes.scholasticahq.com/article/2315.pdf
[7] For an example see Mishnah Nedarim 5:6: https://www.sefaria.org/Mishnah_Nedarim.5.6?lang=bi
[8] https://ourrabbijesus.com/articles/the-soup-nazi-corban-and-jesus/
[9] The NICNT commentary on Mark, pg. 251.

UNDERSTANDING THE SCRIBES AND PHARISEES (VS. 1-4)

WHEN THE SCRIBES AND PHARISEES ARRIVE...

Who all was there?

When did it happen? (Time of day/year)

Where did it happen?

   Coming from/going to?

What happened before/after?

Weather

WHY MIGHT THE DISCIPLES BE EATING WITH UNWASHED HANDS?

WHAT ROLE OR RESPONSIBILITY HAVE THE PHARISEES TAKEN ON IN ISRAEL?

IF THE NEW PASTOR AXED CHRISTMAS, HOW WOULD PEOPLE RESPOND?

THE CONFRONTATION (VS. 5-8)

WHAT'S THE EMOTIONAL CONTENT OF VERSES FIVE TO EIGHT?

WHAT ELSE IS JESUS SAYING BY QUOTING ISAIAH 29?

HOW WOULD YOU RESPOND TO GETTING CHEWED OUT LIKE THIS IF YOU WERE A SCRIBE?

THE CORBAN EXAMPLE (VS. 9-13)
GIVE SOME EXAMPLES OF 'CORBAN' VOWS PEOPLE MIGHT MAKE IN JESUS' TIME.

HUMAN QUESTIONS

HOW WOULD I HAVE FELT?

WHY DID THEY DO THAT?

WHAT WOULD A HUMAN BEING DO?

IF I WERE IN THEIR SHOES...

WHAT EMOTION WAS JESUS FEELING IN THIS PASSAGE?

WHAT INJUSTICE MIGHT JESUS HAVE EXPERIENCED THAT CAUSED HIS STRONG REACTION?

QUESTIONS FOR JESUS

1. Jesus, you had to delay your dream to support your family when your dad died. What was that like for you?

2. What did you feel when you saw your 'boys' being accused of breaking the law?

3. What did you feel growing up when you saw rules being put before people?

4. What deep desire was behind giving us a light yoke to us instead of a heavy one?

ADDITIONAL RESOURCES
Live links to these resources are on-line at: LaHB.net/mark71

THE WRITTEN AND ORAL LAW
"The sages who set about codifying Jewish law classified healing as "work" — it involves the mixing of medicines, travelling to the patient, carrying equipment and other tasks generally forbidden on the Sabbath."
https://www.thejc.com/judaism/all/why-doctors-can-heal-on-shabbat-1.65237

"Our sages taught that a Jew who does not observe Torah and Mitzvot, especially one who desecrates Shabbat, is referred to as a 'wayward Jew.'" https://halachayomit.co.il/en/ReadHalacha.aspx?halachaid=1402

"Wolkenfeld… got her computer programmers on it. It took them 'eight minutes of work and fifteen lines of code' to come up with the answer: 1,860,131 words."
https://www.talmudology.com/jeremybrownmdgmailcom/2019/12/30/berachot-2-how-many-words-are-in-the-babylonian-talmud

"From the first Hebrew word 'B'resh ith' (In the beginning) in Genesis 1:1 to the last word 'Amen' in Revelation, scholars (and computer programs) have counted 443,114 words in the original languages."
https://www.swcs.com.au/BibleTotalWords.htm

HAND WASHING
"The only hand washing required in the OT for purposes of ritual purity is that of priests before offering sacrifice (Ex. 30:18–21; 40:30–32)." NIGTC commentary

"People tend to touch many things (in Hebrew this is phrased—hands are busy) and it would be virtually impossible to prevent one's hands from ever touching something that was impure."
https://www.sefaria.org/English_Explanation_of_Mishnah_Yadayim%2C_Introduction.1?lang=bi&with=all&lang2=en

"The Pharisees believed that all Jews in their ordinary life, and not just the Temple priesthood or Jews visiting the Temple, should observe rules and rituals concerning purification." [i.e. rules Torah only applied to priests]
https://en.wikipedia.org/wiki/Pharisees#Practices

CORBAN
"The person could keep the property in his possession but say to his parents that he cannot offer them any help because he has dedicated it to God" ZIBBC

"But much more likely, a hot-headed young man was arguing with his parents and shouted, 'Corban what I would give you when you are old!'" https://ourrabbijesus.com/articles/the-soup-nazi-corban-and-jesus/

"[Origen] conceded that the interpretation he offered was one of which he would never have thought, had he not learned if from a Jewish informant." https://janes.scholasticahq.com/article/2315.pdf

"An incident occurred involving someone in the city of Beth Horon whose father had vowed not to derive benefit from him…" The Mishnah Nedarim 5:6 https://www.sefaria.org/Mishnah_Nedarim.5.6?lang=bi

How to Read the Bible Like a Human Being | Mark Book Six

THE SYROPHOENICIAN WOMAN
MARK 7:24-30

PASSAGE: MARK 7:24-30 (NASB)

(See also Matthew 15:21-28)

²⁴Jesus got up and went away from there to the region of Tyre. And when He had entered a house, He wanted no one to know of it; yet He could not escape notice. ²⁵But after hearing of Him, a woman whose little daughter had an unclean spirit immediately came and fell at His feet. ²⁶Now the woman was a Gentile, of the Syrophoenician race. And she kept asking Him to cast the demon out of her daughter.

²⁷And He was saying to her, "Let the children be satisfied first, for it is not good to take the children's bread and throw it to the dogs."

²⁸But she answered and said to Him, "Yes, Lord, but even the dogs under the table feed on the children's crumbs."

²⁹And He said to her, "Because of this answer go; the demon has gone out of your daughter." ³⁰And going back to her home, she found the child lying on the bed, the demon having left.

MATTHEW 15:21-28

²¹Jesus went away from there, and withdrew into the district of Tyre and Sidon. ²²And a Canaanite woman from that region came out and began to cry out, saying, "Have mercy on me, Lord, Son of David; my daughter is cruelly demon-possessed." ²³But He did not answer her a word.

And His disciples came and implored Him, saying, "Send her away, because she keeps shouting at us." But He answered and said, "I was sent only to the lost sheep of the house of Israel."

²⁵But she came and began to bow down before Him, saying, "Lord, help me!"

²⁶And He answered and said, "It is not good to take the children's bread and throw it to the dogs."

²⁷But she said, "Yes, Lord; but even the dogs feed on the crumbs which fall from their masters' table."

²⁸Then Jesus said to her, "O woman, your faith is great; it shall be done for you as you wish." And her daughter was healed at once.

BACKGROUND INFO
IS JESUS ACTING LIKE A CHRISTIAN OR A JEW?

If we think of Jesus as a Jew instead of a twenty-first century Western Christian, how does that change this story? Here's a Jewish source explaining what it means to be a Jew:

> *It is important to note that being a Jew has nothing to do with what you believe or what you do. A person born to non-Jewish parents who has not undergone the formal process of conversion but who believes everything that Orthodox Jews believe and observes every law and custom of Judaism is still a non-Jew, even in the eyes of the most liberal movements of Judaism; and a person born to a Jewish mother who is an atheist and never practices the Jewish religion is still a Jew, even in the eyes of the ultra-Orthodox. In this sense,* **Judaism is more like a nationality than like other religions***, and being Jewish is like a citizenship.* [10]

That's almost the polar opposite of the way we think of ourselves as Christians! Yet grasping that difference is vital to understanding this story.

Christianity is a religion defined by beliefs. Anyone can join just by deciding they want to. You don't have to have a certain skin color or change your passport to follow Jesus: your ethnicity has nothing to do with it (see Galatians 3:28). Make a profession of faith, and you are in. So, if the Syrophoenician woman shows up at your twenty-first century American church and begs the elders to pray for her daughter—they would! She is

---

[10] https://www.jewfaq.org/who_is_a_jew

showing faith in Jesus, which is all you have to do to join, so she has standing to make that request. And since to a Christian anyone is a potential citizen of heaven, we'll pray for whoever asks in hopes that they'll join.

But put a Gentile in front of a first-century Jewish rabbi and it's a totally different story. It doesn't matter whether the Syrophoenician woman believes in Jesus. She's not Jewish: not by birth, not as a citizen of the nation of Israel. She's not versed in Jewish culture, and not a formal convert to the Jewish religion. She has no part in what Jesus the rabbi is doing. Judaism is not a multi-ethnic faith: it's more like national citizenship, where you can't vote or get unemployment benefits without a passport.

So, for a Baal-worshipping Greek foreigner to press a Jewish rabbi for the benefits of Jewish citizenship is inappropriate. It would be like the recent scandal where rich white parents gave money to a university to secure scholarships for their less-qualified kids; or if an Irish citizen living in Belfast applied for U.S. Social Security benefits, or an American of European descent falsely claimed to be an American Indian to get access to tribal benefits. In our culture that's the kind of thing you can go to jail for! If the white American says, "'Well, I believe in the Great Spirit," it doesn't make him one-eighth Cherokee. And if the Irishman says, "I've always loved America and American values," that doesn't qualify him for Social Security checks. Judaism reserves its benefits for citizens only, not to whoever has the guts to ask.

One other dynamic to grapple with in this story is how Jews of that day viewed non-Jews. An observant Jew saw other races as unclean, and therefore wouldn't eat with them, refused to enter their homes, would shake the dust off their feet when they left Gentile countries, and certainly wouldn't intermarry with other ethnicities. In modern language, they were racists, like almost all ancient peoples. That Jesus and the early church transcended this to a large degree is quite amazing.

THREE CULTURAL WORLDVIEWS

The world's cultures can be divided into three main types of worldviews:[11]

- **Guilt/Innocence:** individualized cultures that view the world in terms of right and wrong. In these societies we are focused on justice and fairness, enforced by laws. We gain our value from our actions, so guilt is remedied by a counterbalancing action, restitution or apology. Think of America and Western Europe.

- **Honor/Shame:** collectivist cultures that prioritize preserving the honor of the family or community. The focus is on harmonious relationships, and community values are enforced by ostracism or shaming. Personal value is a function of one's standing in the community, and restoring honor can be all but impossible without the intervention of a prominent person. Many Asian cultures fall in this category.

- **Power/Fear:** cultures that see the world in hierarchies and focus on navigating these power structures. People focus on gaining safety and security by appeasing or amassing power, and leadership tends to be authoritarian and use fear to enforce control. The worldview is common in areas with animist religions, highly-structured hierarchies (like the military) or countries with authoritarian governments.

---

[11] Taken from the book, *The 3D Gospel* by Jayson Georges; and https://www.knowledgeworkx.com/post/three-colors-of-worldview

One place these differences come out clearly in the manner in which children are parented and taught. In Western thinking (which is dominated by the **Guilt/Innocence** paradigm), parents are most concerned with imparting to their children the importance of doing what is right, that which is established by rules and law. We emphasize keeping your word, not lying, and other rule-following behaviors. Follow the instructions, stay between the lines, don't do wrong, and apologize if you do! A teacher will get a student's attention by giving them a challenging test and allowing them to fail, for example.

In Asian and Middle-Eastern cultures where the dominant worldview is **Honor/Shame**, the fundamental goal of parents and teachers is to establish that the honor of their family or tribe is paramount. In everything that you do or say, consider how your behavior and words impact the honor of those around you. Do nothing that will bring shame on the family name. If a teacher wants to get their student's attention in class, they will often shame them.

A third worldview common in animistic or authoritarian cultures is **Power/Fear**. Parents and teachers with this worldview are focused on imparting the skills to help children navigate the power structure and hierarchy to keep themselves and their loved ones safe. Children are taught how to achieve and maintain positions of power as well as how to cultivate connections with people of higher position to get what they want. A parent or teacher may use punishment or threat of punishment to get the attention of their student.

Greek, Roman and Hebrew societies of Jesus' time were Honor/Shame cultures. A good example of how this worldview played out in first-century Israel was in the enforcement of the Oral Law. Most of the rulings in the Mishnah have no legal penalties attached to breaking them. To a Westerner from a Guilt/Innocence culture, that seems strange—if there are no fines or jail sentences, how were the rules enforced? In an Honor/Shame culture, compliance is compelled by shame and ostracism from the community.

For instance, on the first day of the month of Adar, the Rabbis went out to examine the fields for what they called 'mixtures'—plants they had ruled should not be intermingled. Instead of instituting a fine to enforce the regulations, they uprooted the plants and publicly threw them at the feet of the landowner—a shaming behavior. In later years they simply uprooted the plants and dumped them on the side of the road in front of the offender's property, where every passerby would see that he had disgraced the whole community.[12] The offending farmer faced loss of status, relationship, and being ostracized if he didn't fall in line.

Since she hailed from the Canaanite city-state of Tyre (which served an animistic religion), the Syrophoenician woman grew up in a Power/Fear culture. Her experience echoed the Roman Patron/client system, where Patrons received honor, loyalty and political support from clients in exchange for protection and favors. It was common practice in the Roman world for a patron to have a sort of 'open-door policy' first thing in the morning where any client could come before him and plead for provision, protection or favors.

As you read this story, try to think through how the woman's behavior was shaped by her Power/Fear worldview, and how it may have clashed with the Honor/Shame worldview of Hebrew society of the day.

---

[12] *Traditions of the Rabbis from the Era of the New Testament*, Vol. I, by David Instone-Brewer, page 216.

JEWISH AND GENTILE CULTURES (VS. 1-4)

ON THE JOURNEY TO TYRE...

Who all was there?

When did it happen? (Time of day/year)

Where did it happen?

    Coming from/going to?

What happened before/after?

Weather

WHY DIDN'T JESUS WANT ANYONE TO KNOW HE WAS IN TOWN?

"SHE KEEPS SHOUTING AT US!"

HOW MANY WAYS CAN YOU NAME THAT HER REQUEST WAS INAPPROPRIATE?

HEAR

SEE

TOUCH

SMELL

TASTE

SECTION II: TWO WORLDVIEWS (VS. 27-30)

WHAT IN THE PASSAGE INDICATES WHETHER THE WOMAN FELT OFFENDED?

WHAT IS THE WOMAN'S CULTURAL WORLDVIEW?

HOW DOES IT CHANGE THE STORY IF JESUS IS INVITING HER INTO A RABBINIC DIALOG?

SECTION II: TWO WORLDVIEWS (CONT'D)

DID JESUS KNOW BEFORE THEIR DIALOG THAT HE WAS GOING TO HEAL THIS WOMAN?

HUMAN QUESTIONS

HOW WOULD I HAVE FELT?

WHY DID THEY DO THAT?

WHAT WOULD A HUMAN BEING DO?

IF I WERE IN THEIR SHOES...

ASSUME JESUS DOESN'T KNOW WHAT TO DO HERE. WHAT DOES THAT EXPLAIN?

WHAT EMOTIONS DO YOU SEE IN JESUS' REPLY IN MATTHEW 15:28?

QUESTIONS FOR JESUS

1. Jesus, were you tired that day?

2. What was it like for you when you got caught between what you understood to be your mission and the need that was standing right in front of you?

3. Jesus, what did you like about this woman's *chutzpah* (boldness)?

4. Have I ever asked you something that changed your mind like this woman did?

ADDITIONAL RESOURCES
NOTE: Live links to these resources are on-line at: LaHB.net/mark724

GREEK AND ROMAN BANQUETS
"The practice at dinner parties was for guests to recline on three large beds placed in a U shape in a triclinium (dining room)." https://blogs.getty.edu/iris/reclining-and-dining-and-drinking-in-ancient-rome/

"Dining was the defining ritual in Roman domestic life, lasting from late afternoon through late at night." https://en.wikipedia.org/wiki/Triclinium

TYRIAN GODS
"Some scholars have identified Moloch with Melqart, a god worshiped in the city of Tyre." https://www.encyclopedia.com/philosophy-and-religion/ancient-religions/ancient-religion/molech

"Human sacrifices, largely children, were also made to appease Melqart at a special site, the Tophet…" https://www.worldhistory.org/Melqart/

"…a hearth was set before a bronze statue of the god Baal (or El) who had outstretched arms on which the victim was placed before falling into the fire." https://www.worldhistory.org/Tophet/

WOMEN IN SOCIETY
"As was common in Roman society, while men had the formal power, women exerted influence behind the scenes." https://www.pbs.org/empires/romans/empire/family.html

"Given that no self-respecting rabbi would deign to speak, let alone converse, with a woman in public, Jesus is showing this woman more than just a little respect." https://gracehb.org/2021/03/the-syrophoenician-woman-the-woman-who-persisted-in-believing-in-jesus-lenten-devotional-3-23-21/

JEWS AND CHRISTIANS
"Judaism is more like a nationality than like other religions, and being Jewish is like a citizenship." https://www.jewfaq.org/who_is_a_jew

"…to be ethnically Gentile (not Jewish) was to be inherently outside of right standing with God." https://www.austingentry.com/meaning-mark-724-30/

CULTURAL WORLDVIEWS
*"In an Honor-Shame–oriented culture, the honor of the family, honor of the tribe, your village, city, the honor of the nation you represent—**honor is key**."* https://www.knowledgeworkx.com/post/three-colors-of-worldview

"A Power/Fear environment… is similar to the patron/client relationships that were present in ancient Greek and Roman societies." https://n-culture.com/blog/45-delving-deeper-into-the-power-fear-worldview

"A friend in Central Asia asked me incredulously, 'Do Americans really eat lunch alone in a cubicle or while driving in the car, like in movies?' Breaking bread together imparts honor, so eating alone is unthinkable." https://honorshame.com/the-5-unwritten-rules-of-honor-shame-cultures/

"The Old Testament contains at least 10 different words, occurring nearly 300 times, to convey various aspects of shame." https://www.pas.rochester.edu/~tim/study/Honor%20and%20Shame%20Tennent.pdf

BONUS MATERIAL | FROM THE BOOK

THE DIFFERENCE A PICTURE MAKES

We all have a set of unconscious pictures of Jesus wedged inside our heads. Those images influence every thought and feeling we have about him, because while our rational brain believes facts, our emotional brain believes pictures.

A great example surfaced while I was leading a group study on the time Jesus met his disciples on a Galilean beach after his resurrection (see John 21:1-14). Jesus tells the disciples to let down their nets in a certain spot, they have a great catch of fish, and John recognizes that it is Jesus. So, Peter puts his clothes on and swims 100 yards to shore to meet him.

Let's try to visualize Jesus' meeting with Peter that day. John (the narrator) doesn't give us any details, since he is 100 yards away on the boat. So, I asked the group to imagine the scene, and we discussed what we could infer: how Peter would be soaking wet and out of breath, how his sodden clothes clung to his body, and how he was tired, cold and hungry after working out on the boat all night. We researched what a beach on that part of the lake looked like, and imagined him jogging up the shingle to stand dripping before a waiting Jesus.

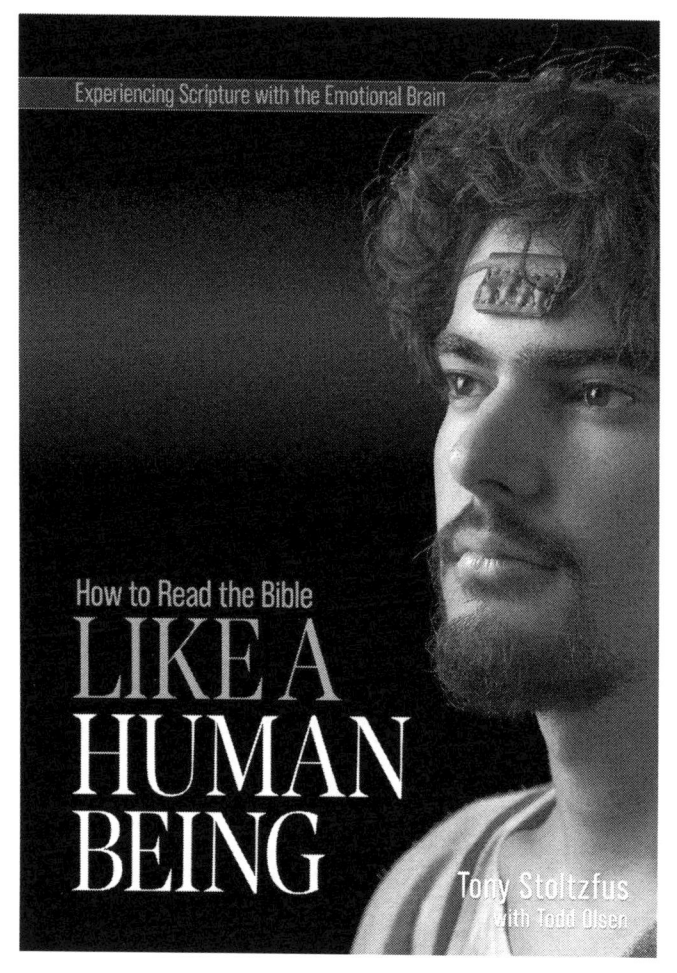

Then my friend Jason spoke up. "You guys are all seeing Jesus standing passively on shore, waiting for Peter to come to him. In my version Jesus is up to his thighs in the lake—he waded halfway in because he couldn't wait to give a huge hug to his best friend."

I was *thunderstruck*. In an instant, I realized that all my pictures of Jesus doing ministry were wrong. In every encounter, I saw the Son of God standing there aloof, with those who sought him covering all the distance between the two of them to make the connection. I saw Jesus standing motionless on the beach, waiting for Peter to swim the whole way from the boat *and* cross the width of the beach to get to him. When they dug a hole through the roof in Capernaum and lowered the paralytic down to Jesus, Jesus didn't help him get out of bed—he just ordered the man to get up and stood waiting for him to comply. At the Pool of Bethesda, I had envisioned Jesus standing over a man lying on the ground, waiting for this individual who was paralyzed to attempt to stand all on his own. I had never pictured Jesus crouching down to the man's level to talk with him, or extending an arm to actually help him up. In all my pictures, it was up to mankind to cross the divide to him.

I remember maybe ten years back having one of those conversations with Jesus where I was apologizing for not spending time with him in the morning. His reply kind of bent my brain: "You know, I can be with you even when you aren't trying to be with me." That was an utterly novel thought—I was so locked into me taking responsibility to come to Jesus in my devotions that in forty years it had never occurred to me that that he might cross the distance to me!

TESTING THE INSIGHT

Today, I firmly believe that Jason was right: Jesus waded in to meet Peter halfway. I am also convinced he extended his hand down to the man at the Pool to lift him up. So, is my conviction based only on a feeling, or merely the opinion of a friend?

No—I fired up my rational brain and tested it! Neither of these stories tell us who closed the distance,[1] but there is another New Testament example that gives a big hint. The first time Peter heals an individual after Jesus' resurrection (see Acts 3:1-8), watch what he does: "And seizing him by the right hand, he raised him up; and immediately his feet and his ankles were strengthened." Disciples in those days were expected to imitate their teacher in everything, down to the smallest personal habits. If Jesus drank coffee with his pinkie extended, a *talmid* (disciple) like Peter would do the same thing. So, by extending a hand down to the man, Peter is probably copying what he'd seen Jesus do!

But there's a deeper reason to think Jesus didn't just stand on the shore with arms folded and wait for Peter. Doctrinally, we are not able to come to God on our own. Adonai took the initiative and covered the distance between heaven and earth by sending his Son. Jason's picture of Jesus wading in to give Peter a thigh-deep hug is a much better match for good theology than my previous one. Where scripture doesn't definitely say one way or the other, aligning my pictures with good doctrine is a much stronger choice!

Refining these mental images is important, because they affect us in powerful ways. The emotional brain believes what it pictures, because that's the only way it can think. So, while my head believed the words I read about Jesus' saving initiative, my heart believed what it saw: that it was my responsibility to cross the distance to God.

When your emotional brain believes one thing and your rational brain believes another, you are doubleminded (the Greek is *di-psychos*, 'two minds'). Knowing a truth in your head but not your heart, like I did with Jesus reaching down to save, creates an internal conflict that prevents you from decisively living out the truth when the pressure is on (see chapter four). In normal, calm circumstances, your rational brain stays in control: you know what the 'right' answer is. But when things get gnarly, the emotional brain engages, those half-conscious pictures in the back of your mind take over, and your rational side gets steamrolled.

To change that, you have to renew *both* your emotional and rational brains. For Western Christians, that means developing new skills for engaging scripture with the underused visual and emotional side of your brain—reading it as story instead as well as theology.

Get the book at www.LaHB.net/thebook

---

[1] The assumption that Jesus just stood there and waited for Peter has no concrete evidence to back it up, either!

Made in the USA
Columbia, SC
04 December 2024